AF668878

Y-431

YOUNG LEARNER'S

LEARNING NUMBERS

1 One Toy

2 Two Clowns

3 Three Ice Creams

4 Four Teddy Bears

5 Five Fishes

6 Six Glasses

7 Seven Gift Boxes

8 Eight Toffees

9 Nine Cakes

10 Ten Apples

11 Eleven Alarm Clocks

12 Twelve Crayons

13 Thirteen Candles

14 Fourteen Party Caps

15 Fifteen Cupcakes

16 Sixteen Spoons

17 Seventeen Balloons

18 Eighteen Butterflies

19 Nineteen Watches

20 Twenty Doughnuts

Activity 1

Match the numbers to their names.

1 •	• thirteen
4 •	• six
6 •	• four
11 •	• fifteen
13 •	• eleven
15 •	• one

Activity 2

Count the objects in each group and match to the correct number.

6 • • 

3 • • 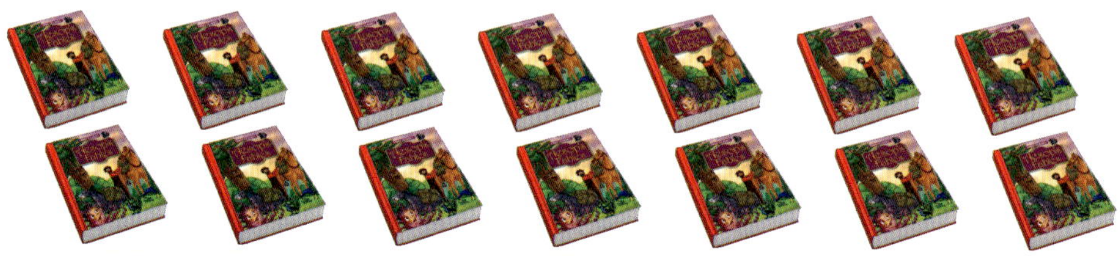

2 • • 

14 • • 

12 • • 

9 • •